A
JACKDAW
SINGS...

'Re-Birth' and Other Poems

Jim O'Leary

ORIGINAL WRITING

Second printing

ISBN: 978-1-908024-08-4

A CIP catalogue for this book is available from the
National Library.

Published by Original Writing Ltd., Dublin, 2011.

Printed by Cahill Printers Limited, Dublin.

For Gerard
with Dear Regards
and Wishes

02/09/2011

Contents

Dedications

This collection of poems, my first, has been some time in the making...not at all because of any shortage of pieces to publish but, actually, because of my own reluctance to lay them bare, so-to-speak, to the world. Over time, my friends and many acquaintances have indulged me by both reading some of my work and enjoying it,...or at least so they said. Always, this has been a sourse of great encouragement to me and I would like to acknowledge that in this dedication.

One person in particular, however, must be singled out for my earnest expression of gratitude. It is really because of her love and support and no small amount of pressure that I have now taken the necessary deep breath and sought to bring my little collection to life. She it is who has been for a considerable time my protector, supporter, life-saver, comforter, and soulmate. She is Trish and I dedicate this book especially to her. In that context, I could not possibly forget Trish's Mum, Toni (Jane) Sisk, (now deceased), a very great lady who was a wonderful friend and surrogate mother to me. Trish features in a number of the poems which relate to different stages of our being together.

I have been blessed with two great daughters, Aileen and Fiona and, in more recent years, with two great sons-in-law, David and Norms. They, in turn, have blessed me with seven grand-children, Sarah, Darragh, Ciara, Sean, Heather, Lilianna and Sophie. I know that each of them will do their best to carry on into the future a little of the best of me and I would like to dedicate this book to them also.

I was born, the eldest of four, to two exceptional people, my parents Paddy and Nora. Both of them passed away many years ago but no day goes by that I do not think kindly of them. Life's environment may well have played a part in shaping me from boy to man and to the present time but I can confidently say that the far greater part of the best of what I am is to their exclusive and eternal credit. I miss them every day.

I was, as I said, the first-born and my celebrated arrival was followed by the arrival of Kate, (Kathleen), Sonny, (Patrick J.), and Mags, (Margaret). The arrival of each of them was likewise celebrated. Always, they have each been stalwarts in support of their older brother and without stint. To each of them, and to their partners, Clare, Paddy and Michael, I say a most sincere thank you.

I have been very fortunate to have had and to have some genuinely great and worthwhile friends without whose care and support I would not have been able to weather the storms and ambushes of life and I thank them each sincerely for being my friend.

Finally, there are four groups who feature in this book about whom I would like to comment. The first is those who, for whatever reason or in whatever circumstances, decided to and did take their own lives. The second relates to all stillborn and miscarried children,...and, of course, their parents. The third, featured in a section of this book as 'About a Man on the Street', relates to those of us who, though cuddled, cosseted and adored as babies, have not been able to withstand the many ambushes and travails of life and who seem to have been let drop through the cracks in the social and economic floorboards,.....the homeless. The fourth group relates to those who meant something to us, whom we valued and who, in so many ways touched our lives and who have passed away. Only a few of that group feature in this book but I like to think that they, for me, represent all of those special people who have gone on before me. Not one person of these four groups should ever be forgotten.

Jim O'Leary

Introduction:
A Boy from the Lodge

The chain clanged as I pulled it through to open the double gate. I struggled with the heavy ironwork, first one side then the other. The car, or van or horse & cart, went through usually with a cursory wave. Sometimes, I got a penny, sometimes a threepenny bit and sometimes nothing at all. Nothing was expected. I was six or seven, I think, and the money was handed up anyway. Afterwards, I closed the gate again. Once through the gates, the vehicles travelled on the avenue toward the Castle or to Milltown, now known as Rathbarry. This gate was an imposing entrance to the Lodge, I often thought as a child. Of course, it didn't belong to us but I could dream. Two enormous pillars framed the big double gate. They were built of stone to what seemed a great height and were crowned by two large stone orbs. There was a smaller pillar of similar design to accommodate the side gate for pedestrians. The side gate was not locked. The magnificent pillars have now suffered the wrath of the elements of time and I think it is a pity that they were not properly maintained. Then, the gates were always closed. Now, they are open to all.

The road from the Lodge toward the Castle was then of gravel and clay drawn from local gravel pits. The surface, an extremely delicate one by todays standards, was well weathered almost on a daily basis by the elements. I well remember the valiant efforts of the local County Council workers to keep the potholes in it at bay. Nevertheless, it served its purpose well enough and it well served the needs of us who used it. Later, stone was crushed to make a more resilient road surface and, of course, tar and stone chippings followed.

We lived in a Lodge which was bought by my parents some time before I was born. I was the eldest of four, born in November, 1943. They bought it, I think, for about eighty pounds which was an absolute fortune then. I have no idea how they managed to pay for it though I have a fair idea that my father sought help from his employer, the local Lisavaird Co-Operative Society, 'The Creamery' as it was then locally called. The Lodge gave entry from the western side, the Ownahincha side, to the Castle and then on to Milltown, (now called Rathbarry). There were a number of other lodges at various points around the Castle grounds which, locally, were called the demesne.

The Castle was the onetime home of the family of Lord Carbery, now long deceased. Rosscarbery was, I believe, named after that family. I have a vague memory of seeing that beautiful Castle fully lit and with music wafting down across the lawn to where, as a young lad, I would sneakingly perch myself at the eastern upstairs window at night. I remember too kneeling at that same window at night when there was a thunder storm to watch the lightning flashes reflecting on the Castle walls. Now, members of the Freke family have made a welcome return to restore what was once a striking and inspiring structure. The Castle was stripped of all of its finery in the early part of the 1950's… I remember that well.

I was immensely proud of that address,...... *'The Western Lodge, Castlefreke, Clonakilty, Co. Cork'*, and I am still to this day. I was the first child of Paddy and Nora O'Leary, (O'Donoghue), delivered at the Hospital in Clonakilty and the Lodge then became my home for a number of very formative years. Three siblings followed to fill the house with new growth and, often as I recall, dreams. It was, I think, a magic place. It is where I came from. That is part of what formed me and made me what I am, such as that is. Then it seemed to me to be a most unique place and, for me, it made us who lived in it unique too.

The Lodge was built of stone, unrendered and unplastered. It had a bay window to the front which favoured, as my mother liked to call it, the parlour. The front door led from a small open porch into what I recall as being a dim and narrow hallway. Downstairs, the parlour was to the left; The hall led to a middle room, the function of which was never clear to me, and then to a very large room which was living room, kitchen and dining room; We called it the kitchen. Behind the kitchen was a back-kitchen, then called the pantry. Upstairs, there were four bedrooms. The large bedroom at the front of the house was where my parents slept. The other three rooms were interconnecting in that the eastern room led to the western bedroom and from that into the back bedroom. There was no bathroom.

The parlour was for visitors only and when not used for that special purpose, it stored anything and everything and was a no-go area for children. It was the place where the milk was put to set so that the cream could be skimmed from it and butter could be churned. Here, everything that needed to be hidden from the children was stored. Here, too, was where the Christmas goodies, including what we called Santy, were hidden from searching eyes….and hands. I well remember discovering a box of Scots Clan chocolate toffees there one Christmas and gorging a lot of them before I was detected. I remember too my sore backside afterwards.

The kitchen, as we called it, was the centre of everything that happened in the house. Here we cooked and dined, washed and studied. A large fireplace, my father's dream and a replication of a beautiful fireplace in the Castle, dominated this room. A large fire was fed from early morning to last thing at night and, often, the warm embers were still glowing in the morning. There was also, in the early days, an old range at which all the baking and cooking for the family was done. This was later replaced by an enamelled Rayburn……or was it a Truburn? I'm not sure now. As I write, I can vividly recall the beautiful and appetising smell of fresh baking, white and brown cakes and, as a treat, a currant cake, each of which would be readily scoffed warm and loaded with butter. My mother could bake! Often, tea bracks, swiss rolls, Madeira cake, currant buns and lip-smacking sponge sandwiches with jam and cream materialised from what would now be described as a very limited kitchen,….nothing in that regard daunted Mammy.

The daily dinner staple was, of course, bacon and cabbage. Fridays were an exception, days on which by edict of the church no meat could be eaten; instead, we had eggs, usually fried, or fish with white sauce both of which were accompanied, of course, by a plentiful helping of boiled potatoes in their jackets. We seldom had fresh fish but I remember enjoying without complaint a decent feed of dried and salted ling which had to be soaked overnight before boiling it; this was served with a white sauce made from cornflour and heavily laced with onions. Sundays, too, were an exception. Breakfast, which every day consisted of tea, brown bread and a boiled egg,…with porridge in winter,…was replaced with a fry, after Mass of course, on Sunday morning. Fried eggs, rashers with stubble still on the skin and the famous Donnellys skinless sausages were our Sunday luxury. Usually, a roast joint of beef or a boiled leg of mutton would be presented for the dinner. Either joint often served as a cold dinner or supper offering on the Monday. The mutton was boiled with a substantial quantity of pearl barley added and the juice left after the meat was removed made a most tasty soup.

The kitchen was also the social centre of the house. There was no television then. We had a ring board with twelve numbered hooks with six rubber rings which was permanently fixed to the kitchen door and which was put to regular use by both children and adults, including visitors. At Christmas, a large balloon would be blown up and we all participated in a game a bit like volleyball in which, if you let the balloon touch the floor, you were in trouble. It was to this room that all visitors, except those designated as 'special' by my mother, were brought. 'Special' visitors, of whose arrival my mother had adequate notice, were brought to the parlour from which, in advance, everything inappropriate according to my mother would have been stowed out of sight. 'Stowed' was one of Mammy's favourite words,...everything had to be 'stowed'. In the kitchen, you were served the regular daily fare of the family. The parlour was different. There, visitors were fed treats the likes of which were rarely then seen.....special biscuits, cakes and sandwiches and such like. Leftovers, when the visitors were gone, would be eagerly sought but little was usually left. We could dream and salivate but to no avail.

I attended at Rathbarry, some times then called Kilkerran, Primary School which was about two miles or so from the Lodge. I started at the old school when I was approaching five years old. The old school consisted of two rooms, one for the lower classes and the other for the higher classes, and with outside toilets. The rooms were basic and with little comforts except for a fire in each room either for the teachers or the pupils. The toilets, one male and one female, were no more than small sheds with a shuttered off front and long wooden seats with holes in them. Through these holes we delivered as we needed onto a steadily rising and smelly heap. I assume, because I never checked, that the girls were provided with a similar facility. It was basic but it, somehow, served the purpose and the fact was that we, then, had no greater expectation.

We brought lunch to school which consisted, usually, of bread and jam sandwiches with a recycled glass bottle filled to the brim with tea or cocoa. The bottles were placed close to the fire to be kept warm and, sometimes, they became so hot that some of them burst. That created an enjoyable diversion as well as a source of annoyance for the Master. Lunchtime was spent in the yard which had a rough unpaved surface. Some of us were rough enough for it though some were not. Games were simple and limited. Football, or our version of it, was played with a tightly tied ball of paper or with, on a rare occasion, a goats bladder well blown up and tied securely. Mostly, we ran around not really having any idea of anything else. Later, a new school was built to the west of the old one. I think that I had then moved up to Master Griffin's room. I suppose this new building was, at the time, state-of-the-art but this made little difference to any of us. It was weather-proof, of course, and had sheds where shelter could be found but our activities remained more-or-less unchanged. The yards were concreted and allowed for less hazardous play.

I had two teachers, Master Griffin and Miss Crowley. I started with Miss Crowley and 'graduated' inevitably to Master Griffin. I have good memories of both of them. Teaching was tough then. Facilities were effectively non-existent and everything came down to the abilities and skills of the teachers. Miss Crowley taught the junior classes up to, I think, second class. During this period, we 'made' our First Holy Communion. After that, we had the Master! Now, things got really serious. He taught four classes, third, fourth, fifth and sixth, in the course of which we 'made' our Confirmation. To bring our primary education to a close, we were required to sit the State Primary Examination. The Master took his responsibilities in these matters particularly seriously and I think it is fair to say that we were well prepared, or as well as we allowed, for both. Sometimes, the measure of that seriousness was the liberal wielding of a long stick cut in the local woods and carefully pared and prepared. We knew his form. The redness of his nose was, for us, the barometer of that form for the day. Sometimes, we got it right but not always. Sometimes, we escaped his ire and the stick but not always. Of course, we thought him to be a cruel man on many an occasion but, nonetheless, I remember him very kindly. His teaching was faultless although the manner of it might, sometimes, have been more tender but there was little tenderness to be had in those times. I have much to thank both of those teachers for and I believe that they played a great part in engraining in me the desire and appetite which, when I ultimately recognised them in myself, enabled me to really learn and to continue to seek learning.

School finished at three o' clock and I walked home to the Lodge. Lessons had to be done then amid the various other necessary, sometimes noisy, activities of the household. There was no separate or dedicated area for study and you simply sat at the kitchen table and got the work done. Of course, there was also other work to be done. Outhouses had to be cleaned out and bedding brought in for the animals. We had a few cows and there were always a few sows and fattening bonhams. Water had to be drawn from the well which was some distance away in the Castle lawn and it was only when all work was done that supper was eaten. In the early years, it was straight to bed after supper although we often hid silently on the turn of the stairs to listen in to conversations if visitors arrived. As we grew up, we were allowed to stay up later and it was then that we started to learn to play games such as Ludo and Snakes & Ladders; card games were not allowed. Then, too, we were allowed to listen to the radio and, sometimes, to stay up when there were visitors. At the weekend, we had some greater latitude in that we were allowed to listen to Radio Luxembourg but, all too soon, the weekend was over and it was back to school on Monday morning.

I left the Lodge at the age of eleven going on twelve when, in September, 1955, I was sent off to boarding school. I was, we all thought then, going to be a priest. The school was the African Mission College, Ballinafad, near Castlebar in County Mayo. Though it has long ago ceased to be a school or college and is now idle and unused, the college still stands despite my best juvenile efforts then. Now, I really had to behave myself! Now, I had to be almost saintly and a constantly dedicated little man of the Church and, by God, I was that occasionally because that was the best I could muster. To make matters worse, I returned at the end of my first term at College to a new home, the home of my Grand-Uncle, locally known as 'The Master', to which, in the meantime, my parents and siblings had moved. The new house…,it wasn't new at all…, was a typical two storey country house with three bedrooms and, again, no bathroom. We had an outside toilet but we did wash indoors. It lacked the many nooks and crannies and, of course, it lacked the character of the Lodge but it was now, once and for all, to be my home. I yearned and mourned for that Lodge but I had left now its safe and wholesome environs hehind forever…….actually, I have never really left that beautiful and forming place and I still hold its many memories close in my age-ing heart!

(To be Continued,…..Maybe!)

Re-Birth

A scent of fear
but knowing no fear
or knowing no need for fear,
I floated in embryo
en-wombed in a swim for life.....
.....I was a miracle,
a wonder of the world,
I know that now.
Creation manifest in me
a Master's touch, whatever called;
No chipped technology ever had such skill;
My parents did,
embraced,
split the atom, so to speak,
and made me;
Now they're gone
and I must live with memories.
I was a wonder once
close to drowning and then born,
a miracle, I know that now,.......
….....…….......How have I done?

BITS & PIECES

A Dream...

Golden strands
Flowing
Past shoulders
To her waist
Almost
Shimmer
In a passion-
-Flow embrace
Begging for
Response,
She looked,
Did she
Or was she
Thinking,
Smiling,
Wondering
Perhaps,
Or not
But she looked
And smiled
Or did she
And was I
There at all,.....
......I wonder!

BRING GRAN!

Stranded hair,
ridged face,
frayed legs,
the old lady
tensed her way
through a family
holiday meal
of three generations
in Blarney,
County Cork,
Ireland
and I wondered
who the outing was really for!

C'EST LA VIE!

I came
When Fate allowed
And left the past behind;
I looked
Accross the wall
And saw a stone-way through;
I stepped
Over the wall
And landed
In a heap of shit;
I came
And saw
And stepped
And wanted to go back
But I was stuck again!

CASABLANCA

Shag off, you asshole,
The stage is mine
 And the piano is for Sam
As in the film;
If you don't,
I'll play your death
In Casablanca,
An end-song,
Play it again, Sam;

Beat the keys
And flap your fingers,
Sit at the piano
Like a tin-pan alley-man
Playing a tune of death,
A distant drum,
A song for me and Sam
And I am there
In black and white,
A dream,
And we're all dead
But I will watch the film again!

Deep Breath

"Kitchen help wanted,
apply within",
the piece of paper
in the window said;

the restaurant was Italian
and posh enough,
too posh for him
in his track-suit bottoms
and flip-flops,
but he went in;

his gut quivered
as he faced the place,
the waitress and an alien menu
daunting him for a second;

he funked
the application
for a while
and ordered lunch
to help his cause...
...and then he asked.

CANCER

She fought the battle and the war
And I looked on from the beginning;

I never knew
There was a war
Only a battle;
The question-mark
With no solution
Arrived unwarned
With unrelenting haste
And hunger
Discounting her at will
And me;

I watched
Unarmed to meet the test
Took no part in the battle
Merely looked
It seemed forever.….
……..then she lost the war.

E.T.

I heard the rumble in the distant night
And wondered;
It was strange
No plane could make that noise
And this is not the San Andreas fault
So there's no earthquake coming;
The sound came close,
The ringing in my ears
Became a turbined pressure
Singling out my mind
From room and body
Taking over consciousness;
My first thought was to say
It can't be them.
Why did I think so.
What a stupid nightmare;
Then I lifted from the chair
And floated
To an endless dream with them.

ALCOHOLISM

It's alright
I'll have
another
one
Tonight,
Just one
And then
I'll go to bed
for now!

Don't Forget the People!

Walk on the path of fortune to the end of emptiness;
run to the bank of hope, a misguided dream;
take a journey to the world with the promise of its trappings
and the winds of time will tell the story of a failed endeavour.

Take the path of Freedom
on a People journey-dream
and a tempered doing;
walk on the fringe of Hope
and forgotten Dreams
and the Sun-face of the World will turn;
give
and the dream-face of the World,
of Real People,
will return the coin;
stay
with the Heart and Soul of you,
of Value,
and the Real-World will live,…..
…..where is the human-world without the Human?

Happy People,......Now?

Set in the fall-below
Of a world-decline,
A couple spar for another day;
Sleep is lost
In a desperate
Scream for ease
But nothing comes,
The power-boys
Have had their way;
No room to move,
He shoves, she shifts
To find a glimpse of light,
A glimmer even,
That will soften
Their tomorrow
But the lads,
The biggest guns around,
Have stripped
The cupboard bare......
.....Slowly in a wearying world,
They sink
Through a quagmire of despair
Where life cannot be kept intact
And happy disappears
Into a chasm.

Honk Off!

The nose is a strange appliance,
a projection of flesh
picking its way
and leading its bearer
on a preoccupation
with an idle finger;

"He's having a pick",
they'd say,
pretending not to look
but unable to resist
his enjoyment,.......
.......they do it too!

HOOKER

"Fuck off....
...What do you think I am?"
She knocked
On the car window
Others lingered
Posed on the street,
Exposed;
"Do you want....."
"What" I asked, not hearing
as I opened the car window;
"Do you.....I have a place nearby".
I look to side and back,
The car in front has moved,
I move a few feet,
Not more.
"I'm clean and cheap" she said,
"and I'll go with you now";

I look again
To left and right and back
Who knows me here;
If she sits in
Who'll know
But what about my car,
The hidden cameras, maybe,
And the other drivers;
I look again,
Head down to hide my face,
Take off my steaming glasses,
Ask how much
And quickly take her in......
.........Fuck them!

Dragging Feet in the Heat

Footsore
In a City jungle
I looked at my feet
And wondered
If they were meant
For this;
Morning
Was a good time
But the mid-day Sun
Crept through my veins
And gorged my energy;
I was spent
Before I started,
A crippling trek
Was more
than I could face,
So I sidled
Back to the hotel
And went to sleep!

Special Needs in the Restaurant

Nowhere, or else not here,
The boy, a welcome spasm-attack
On the shabby fitters-in,
Put his simple imagination
To a riddle foody-test
As those shitty-people
Posed at a party-plan
And rehearsed their precious world;

The boy, an embrace of Mam,
Sprang here and there
With eyes that did not look
But with enthusiastic grace
Took the whole world
In his limit-look
A manifest
Of his affliction
And enlightened
A bewildered world
With his grasp of reality,
The wonder-boy was real!

Its All The One

I wanted to be
The one
Who carried
Cowdung on my shoes
Into the Four-Star Restaurant
But I didn't
And I brought my friends
Instead for dinner......
,,,,,,SHIT.

Keep it for Yourself!

A dog-shit landed
On the beach
And the dog-man
Walked away;
Dog Shit,
I hear a scream
Unheard by him
As he left for home;
Don't shit on the beach, dog,
For me or anyone,
Take it home for the dog-man
To embrace;
It is yours and his, not mine
And not for me
Or for the beach,…..
…..Shit athome , please!

LAST ORDERS

He squeezed
the last drop,
spat and pissed
enjoying the process;

Pissed,
the thought
became
a sobering glimpse
of sanity
but he pressed on
and puked
to make more space
and later
pissed for pain
and squeezed the last drop,
spat
and hoped for more,…
….he was the last to leave alone!

MALE MENOPAUSE

He sits
And travels in his mind,
Beautiful faces haunting him
Young faces drawing him
To interludes of emotion
None complete
But each with promise,
Vague,
And still he sits alone;
He is free
But bound unfree
And yearning
For lost-time fulfilled
He travels,
Mind unbound,
Through stretches of imagined
And complete consuming
And, without the fetter
Of a dulled emotion
Chaining him,
Makes love
Without the love
To be still free.

MURDER ON THE MED

I sat by the pool,
Something I rarely do,
And viewed the rock-face
Leaning upward to its edge;
At the top, I saw a couple,
Young-entwined
but somehow prickly,
Sharp-words coming
In the breeze,
Floating down to me below;
He, a swarthy
Sallow-colour,
Held her arm,
His eyes on her
Enthralled with spite
Coupled for a second
Or so with hers
To press to her
His need,
Then I saw him push;

She fell the distance
To the rock below
Yards from my face,
A shocking thump,
Then he was gone
And she and I were left alone!

PARTY TIME

Party time
Screams abounding
Lapses waiting to embrace
The limpid drunken forms
Of a world in sickness
And the People wait
For the Puking
Sick to come;
In the dark light
Waiting moment
Settled people
Wait to take their bait
But, alight with flame,
Their dung-breath dream
Of sodden shots
Regurgitates
And chokes alive
Their menace;
Snuggled down
In an adept cover-space,
Home-based Party-People
Who know the form
Slam the window, close the blind
And leave their sick to them;

The night is a dark place
For many with the fear
Of noise and night is filled
With the dread
Of the worst of it
That's still to come
And come they will
Determined with their
Puking savagery
To rape our well-earned sleep;
I will take revenge
On the sick-mind pukers
Of my world, the place
Where I must live
Until they're gone
Or I have Killed them
Or until I've sucked
Their Souls from them,…..
…..It is for that I wait,
And I'll survive!

Spellbound

She is the daytime hare,
A beauty of the dark;
He is an eagle of the night
Mortal by day;
As sunlight dims
The hare becomes the beauty
And the man soars delta-winged
into the sky;
Condemned, they search
Through endless time
For unbewitching spell
And failing,
The eagle steals the whisper of the wind,
Fly-dives into her comfort-breast of earth
And no more pain....
......And they live on in dream.

Puppy Love 1

A still-new ache
And pulsing sharp,
A poignant pain
Eroding common sense
Yet not rejected,
Clings instead
To trauma-burden
Prolonging hurt intense
Vainly, perhaps,
But borne,
Mind's dream,
Yearning
A kindred-dream reply.

Puppy Love 2

The bell proclaims
A time for fleeting ardour
When soul meets soul
In silent-hope exchange;
The time is short
And silence suspends tension
But not enough
To quell the pain;
When silence breaks
A dialogue of sharing
Cleaves to the core of privacy
Then lapses to another calm;
This cameo-succession
Of silence touching silence
Preserves a cycle of enquiry
With a longing-hint implied
That the next call might herald
The return of sharing;

But time is gone
And waiting yields
To apprehension
Logging days by hour
The hours by minute
Waiting in a harsh uncertainty
For the next call
A promise
Of awaited balm,…..
…..But there's no call!

AN ENCHANTED CYCLE

Clasped safe within a steep-walled cove
The world outside is somewhere but not here;

A sheer rock-face
On either side
Presents a cushioned
And embracing screen
Meeting one end in apex
And opening a triangle to the sea;

The rock-walls frame
What feels like, is a heaven bed
Where noone, nothing
Or adversity can touch
And squinting windows
Have no place,
Where touching stars
Can find escape to dream;
Tide at one end
And the other of the day
Leave in between a life-span
It seems for lovers
Safe within a rock-wall
And a sea-embrace;

The sand-bed grows
As the high tide ebbs
And the water grows again
To sink the sand-quilt
Where two lovers lie in one,
A moment of eternity,
And the sea will leave
No place for them
Except the certainty
That their cycle will endure;

As the waters grow
From the sea-belly
The two spirits
Must part and leave,
The ocean swells
Toward the narrow cove,
A waiting haven,
And drives impassioned,
Engorged to a sea-penis,
It presses and penetrates

The vulval walls in rhythm
Again
Again
Again 'til spent
And recedes
Then calmly fulfilled
Leaving behind
A sated glistening;

Two spirits
Watch from the cliff-top
Wanting waiting
And then again
They take back
Their special space.

THE KISS

Deadwood drifted in a bog alone
And it was lost for years;

Drag the waters for a life-line
Search for a wild flower bed
Seek the sea-washed sand for feeling
And find tomorrow every day;
Dig the trenches for protection
Find the cover of their earthen warmth
Call the Gods to make a heaven-spread
Discrete screen for love;

Deadwood in a simple life-form
Singled out by a hand-caress
Found the soulmate of a lifetime,
Embraced its finding hands,
And kissed all the pain goodbye.

At Last

Snow freckles
Flirting in a merry dance
A thousand-fold
Mesmerise the wind
As they fall in playful flight
Flitting here and there
Until they touch
Where they belong;
Alone each flake is nothing
In a pale-consuming world
Together once they touch
They are fulfilled...
...they are enough.

THE STRAND

A sea of sand stretches
From the Galley Head
Washed day by day
Into a plaster-board;
Glistening here and there
It throws a wall
Of no avail
Against the throb of rising tide;
At night a shaft of light
Spans countryside
And flickers in phase
From a quartz-mix
Sending a tidal message
A despatch of cosmic influence;
It stretches for a mile or more,
A long strand edged by a frame
Of mile-long reed-held dunes
And children paddle
In its salt-drenched table
Picking fancy stones to treasure;

I watch and know
That long strand will endure
But I will not.

WAITING FOR CLIONA

A fin cleaves through the waves
Cutting a shimmering path
In nature's endless dream,
A dorsal, maybe a shark
Intent on prey of fish or flesh
The vicious circle of the sea or mystery?
Is it real or a mirage
Or is it Cliona come to visit
Her rock-bed in moist-weld draped
Seeking, perhaps, a scaled embrace?

I wait and watch
Bent on a fatal prospect
She takes young men they say
But none she took came back to tell;
Who will she take
This time and when
Noone perhaps this century
And still I wait
Maybe this time she'll lay
On her love-rock with an older man
And, finished, take him, me,
Into her sea of dreams,…
…That's why I wait!

In the Jervis Centre, Dublin

Pacing wondering
Thoughts fucked up
By savage words
And fear of fear,
The thought, and
Fear came readily
Sleeping
Shopping
Going to the brink
Of an embrace,
He waited,
Wanted, yearned for
What he thought was good
And then he pissed
And gave it all away,…
…There's no more left.

In Memory of all Still-born and Miscarried Children

She faced
A grumpy morning
Sick but hoping
For the life in her;
The pain would not relent,
Her hope escaped,
Her embryo
A thumb-nail piece of life
In early-form
Left her helpless
To avoid existence,
She miscarried
And her child-dream died.

UNDER THE CRYSTAL BALL

I moved against her,
She pressed on me
And we danced;
I'm inside you now, I said
and she replied
And I'm around you
Wrapped,
Enveloping you in me,
Your being inside,
And we could not be more
Together;
Dancing, not dancing,
Barely moving
And joined
Deep in our skin caress,
A flowing sense,
We dreamed;
Dancing, not dancing,
We came
Together once,
Again,
And we could not be more
Together,
Forever....
....under the Crystal Ball.

Where have all the Flowers Gone

Take me to the bushes
To the crinkly warmth
Of heather on my bum
Back to forgotten days
For some but not for me
When you and I made love
As we walked the streets
In wistful dream;

I know the bridge is gone
Replaced by a tarmac-runway
And horse-power drives
A trench mile-wide
Through nooks of memory;
The dance-hall light is quenched
Where once we clung
Enraptured in orgasmic smile,
We hugged, caressed
And loved excluding everyone;

The years have flown
Past you and I
And taken toll of
Memory and muscle,
Quenched the one
And sapped the other;
Lapsed time has warned
There's no more time
So take me to the bushes
And press me firm
To crinkly warmth of heather
Back to forgotten days
When young love dreamed
And saw no consequence
Of lapsing time
And we made love;
Will you and I
Again make love
As we walk the streets
Or will we ever meet at all.

THERE'S A PLACE.......

Roses are red
And violets are blue
the blue and red together
make up green
the colour of the world
and the green is the bluebell-bed
of trees
and of buttercups and primroses
and white-winged yellow-centred daisies
and garlic
and noone walks the fields
and the sun shines through the woods
in tunnels
to light a beam-base space for lovers
where they will find a darkness-comfort
and a glow
and they will rest together
on a carpet of wild flowers
and they will walk unseen together
on a seamless comfort-turf
leaving footprints there forever
in the flowers and the ground
then they will be forever
enough.

CREATION

Slate upon slate,
Glued with a rough-hand,
Erupted in the structure
Of a lamp,
Rose in the dark
From a barren-base;
Touch the earth core,
The mason whispered
To himself as his chisel cleared
And the hammer,
Directed by his mind-bent,
Tapped a tune, a-drawing
Symmetry with stone;

It began in darkness,
Piece by piece in a spiral pace,
And from the earth
An embryo-work unfolded
And the wonder was a miracle
Flowing from the mason's hands;
Touch the core,
The slate-man shouted to the world
As the thing took shape
And he wondered at its beauty
And its source
But the finished work
Would herald its conception....
....the world
is a wonder everyday.

Hedge Funds

I woke up one fine Summer morning
My resources were stripped to the bone
And intent on avoiding a panic
I decided to call the bank on the phone;
The girl put me through to the Manager
And I asked for a small overdraft
He sneered and he snorted and sniggered
And said that he was not that daft;
Distraught, I looked 'round my little hovel
My grey cells were racing like hell
I ransacked the place with a vengeance
But found that I had nothing to sell;
Despondent, I tidied the place up
Realising that no money no fun
When glancing at a cluttered corner
I noticed my Grandson's toy gun;
Ah Ha, I shouted out with some glee
As a plan began to form in my head
The bank's floor will be awash with pee
When they think that my gun's full of lead;
The morning broke clear and serene
As I wound myself up into action
And I made my way to the bank's door
Abrim with a dosh-driven passion;

With a note in my hand and my gun tucked away
I slid toward the counter as they started their day
Showing the gun and the note with a confident dash
I demanded a shit-load of cash;
Well, the dough was forthcoming in double-quick time
And I grabbed it and trousered it quickly
Then skipping lighthearted endowed as I then was
I slipped from the bank's clutches safely;
Then I strolled down the street
With a lift in my step
And I gloated on the part I had played,
Gleaned without any graft
I now had my overdraft
And no interest would have to be paid,...
....The banking class
Can kiss my arse
I've got my overdraft at last!

HOSTAGE

I am a bush in a clump of bushes
Rustling in the breeze alone;
I am a tree reaching to the clouds
Mature, full grown;
I am the grass around tree and bush,
A soft-bed for the world,
A lake of mirrored sheen,
A resorvoir of tears,
A day of expectation
In a sea of stormy time.

I am a dolphin of the deep
Searching shallows for response,
The tree and bush, the grass,
The lake of tears unseen,
Unheard in time and space,
A pawn;
I am the world and nothing,
A shadow hovering, waiting
On the careless hand of fate
And her reply.

LOVE ON A MOONBEAM

A soft breeze whispered
Through the window-screen
The room inside was lit
By its sweet sound;
Moonlight flowed
With its airborne glitter
And the early air
Was crisp and clear;
A soft breath whispered
In her silken ear,
Her face was blushed
With its fragrance;
Smile on smile
Followed the breeze
And the moonlight
Embalmed her soul;

Sometimes
When the curtains stirred
Her room was cooled
And nothing moved;
Sometimes when the night
Had closed around her
And the coolness grasped
Her heart and soul
He whispered sweetness
On the breeze to her

And she was warm
And well;
Sometimes
When he touched her skin,
Brushed his fingers on her cheek,
She heard his silent whispers;
Sometimes
When he called
She felt his arms enwrap her
In a life embrace;

Always
In their nearness
When they touched
Or not
That whispered love
Was there for them;
Always
Reaching
Always
They are one.

POEM TO ME...

I'm here but not my own space,
The place where I am home,
And the settled form of me
Is waiting for a foe to come,
To ambush that earthly sod
Where I am firmly rooted
In the soil from where I came,
From where I was created;

Savage me
If you will
But the best of you
Will not
Defeat
The best of me;
Take your best shot
And be gone,...
I will weather that
And survive;
The World
Is a strange place
So, look at my World
To see what's really me
Before you take
Your shot!

Nights Promise

A thumb-nail moon
Lit the grass,
The blooms reflected
A tomorrow life;
Pansies folded
In their blossom-sleep
And the lavender
Worked its wonders;
I was lost in your place,
In the colour-scape of you,
My life-blood speeding
Past my years;

I scanned the spectrum of your 'garden'
And its landscape merged in my soul;
I took the image of your shape and hew
And I slept and dreamed..........

Old Friends

I remember
The horse-drawn plough,
I am older now;
The best has come and gone
But image lives
Where furrows with the years
Have grown
And the horse is gone;
I saw the clotted bands
Turned gently
Behind the iron cleaver
Line by line
By the horse, drawing,
Guiding hoof by hoof,
A swirl of seagull
On his tail;
I heard the cacaphony,
Sometimes in tune,
Some not,
In worm pursuit,
A symmetry of wings
Forming a halo-crest

Headland to end and back;
Today, we reminisced,
My friend and I,
Both old sinse then,
Talked of grasshoppers
And neighbours,
Of things
no longer known,
And neither knew
If our memory-treasures
Would again be found
But we remembered.

ELEVATION OF THE HEART
(The Destiny of an Irish Immigrant to America)

Abroad in the swamp-land,
A sinking ground of people,
the simple-man embraced
a wonder of the world
of wondrous promise
and he kept the Faith;
Prospering in that vein,
He waited, fought his way
And set the path for his avail
With a hope that bought
No thought of failure;
He had the promise
Of a world, the World
That brooked no vacuum
With its gold in place
For him to take,…
….it was promised
and his destiny to take
but it went wrong
and the devils took the reins
of his brave venture
when his people died,
his World and future dead,
when the shit-planes hit the towers;

Dead and ashes,
Dead and buried
Mattered not a lot
When the world
Was burned
Into a cinder-space;

The next step was
A spectre-plot
Where voyeurs might come
To view a corpse or smell of it,
The end and death of life,
the killing, life expired,
of many many loves
who'd never been before
And killing never stopped,
The World refused to see
That people,
Children, babies, old as well,
Were fodder
For their kill-machines
And still,
In flesh-fed smoke
The lives of all
Were being spent,
The World was coming to an end for all of them
And Hope was lost, abandoned in that wake!

Gentile or Jew,
The deaths continue
year by year,
For decades and a time
Until we saw that lives
and life should live
Despite the havok
Of the savage zealots
And a wishful World
Began to seek relief
Of Peace not War
For the children
of the rest of us,…
…what else is there for anyone?

A War Ghost

The Great Wars
1914 to 1918
And 1939 to 1945
Swept the world
And nothing ever
Was the same again;
Children of the Cities
Of the best of Europe
East and West were killed
And the frenzy said
That in its drive 'twas for the best,
I felt today that it was not;

In Nice, the old City,
I passed, by accident,
A Memorial
To the dead of Wars,
The Great Wars
That left so many marked
And not just here
But everywhere;

The taxi skimmed around
In a stream of going cars
To there and everywhere
But next was my Hotel
And I knew that I could not
Go home or anywhere
Without going back
To meld with what was there;

So, rapt, I went to stand
At the vigil for their dying,
Their leaving life for man
And life for me
And I sat to the edge
Of their now Monastery,
A place to worship them
For me and anyone;
The lights were dim,
The Sun had settled low,
And a wispy dream-like fog
Rose from the grass
At their dedicated place,
That place to which
I now felt drawn
And then he came;

The ghost of a Soldier, 1914-1918, appeared
His story is told in short little shimmers of words
Until, at last, he says "I'm your Grandfather, Boy,
You have a brother called after me";
"What's your name", I asked.
And "Sonny", he replied;
As the evening noises
Swept up on the breeze,
I thought of my only brother, also Sonny,
In Nice on the 15th of August, 2009;

I heard the fireworks
Crackle and bump and boom
And I needed to be near
The monument
That Monastery, for them
Who heard it all before
The battle noise
The wounds of their encounters;

"My name is Sonny", he said;
All I could see was mist,
The smog of fireworks,
maybe battle,.....I wondered!
"My name is Sonny,
I think I know you";
I stopped a distance
from the monument,
the notice said be quiet
and show respect
And I acknowledged that;
His shape persisted,
the smog of battle, fireworks maybe,
seemed to waft toward the sea
but my eyes were drawn
to the spot, that spot
where his fog-bound form appeared;
I was rooted there,
My early life
Appearing
In an envelope
Of generations,
My mother's father,
Daddy, Grandad, gone
and now come back, I thought,
and then I cried in the memories

Of the stories I'd been told;
I am but a boy,
of many dreams,
of shapes and tying shoelaces,
A boy with nothing
but a wealthy store of mother, his child,
The baby of her mother left behind;
I looked at all of this and wanted to embrace
his squandered soul for me;

The ghost came on
And with him came
A smell of cordite,
The stink of battle,
that smell to push the soldier
to let life go
and to appear just once
again in living flesh;
"My name is Sonny',
he cried again to me
And as he faded
I was pressed to smile;

"My name is Sonny",
he then whispered,
"I am your mothers father,
your grandfather, Son"
and I knew that he was here
for me and for my brother, Sonny,…..
"I'm glad to meet you", he said
as he drifted from my view.

(In Memoriam Patrich Joseph, (Sonny), O'Donoghue, RIP,
My Grandfather)

AND WILL I BRING MY CAP, GIRL........?

Will I bring my cap,
Girl?
I will
But I cannot think..
..Will it rain or not
Or will we wait
To see
If we might see the world
Before the rain comes.....
.....I'll wait
But will you look for me
Because if rain comes
I'll get wet
and I have no mind
to escape or to be dry....
.....I am sorry
but I'm lost,
A simple sorry fool,
Gone
To Alzheimers...
...and I am lost.

My Boy is Dying

My boy is dying,
Slipping
Slowly away
From me,
An old man,
His prime intact
But mine
Long gone,
My time to go
Long gone;
Why am I
Still here
Why must I
Survive
To see that loss;

My boy is dying
And will soon be gone.

(For Little William)

The Mother was Angry...

Forty years or so
With Paddy
Stitched together
By good times
Adversity
And soul
Nora was
In pride
And humble
Measures
Worth acclaim
She thought
And right she was
In that belief;
Anger was a waste
She said to me, to many
From the centre of her being
In her best sincerity;
Once or twice
In hasty moments
Seldom seen
She reached an edge
That could belie
Her stated calm;

Once only, though,
She slipped
The hold of her proclaim
When Paddy,
Boldened with a whiskey,
Spoke to their guests his pride
In Nora's admired features
And announced
That she should look so well
With the price
Of a calf's bounty
In her mouth;
The mother was angry then
As never seen before
And Paddy paid
A well-earned price,
A penalty embraced
With gracious fear
To sooth my mother's ire,…
…The lesson gravely taught
Was not to be forgotten.

BY THE LAKE

Back to the start
He took you there
And talked of all there was
Of his beginning
Of what was between the then
And now of everything
From his home-lodge
And castle view
And what went on inside
His safe home-base and him;
He talked of birth and growing
And his walk to school age four
And trees and barefoot dancing
Through the woods of nature-love
And seeing everything
The grass, the lake, the trees,
(all gone),
The castle raped
A drive-through
Of past lives of him;
He took you to the start of him
And found for you and him
A time and space alone
And both of you were one,
Are one together
By that lake of special dreams.

Idol

Stone centred
On an oaken pedestal
A barren cushion barefaced
Enclosed in verdigris
Ornamented the world
Inanimate and heartless
Despite the warmth outside and in
And treasured in admiring waves;
When she was asleep
The statue alive
Would come to her
In warming silence
And leave again in darkness
For his cold base;
He wanted to be warm
Not loveless stone
But could not speak it
Confined
On his barren cushion
An ornament
Feeling the world
In heart and soul
Not stone
And waiting
Biding on his plinth;
Warming to his need to speak
He rested and resolved

In his icon-mind
To confront his fate
And speak,…...
…...But she was gone.

I was a Thief....just once

I walked into the large shop
With bits and pieces everywhere
The selection was beyond me
And I couldn't believe my luck;

I was seventy yesterday
I had no birthday party
The kids are gone
The husband too
And noone came
No cards or gifts came either,
I was seventy yesterday
And the world ignored my day;

This morning I remembered every day
And all my birthdays gone,
The cards and presents,
The calls that did not come,
And I wondered how I'd celebrate
My day of days, my birthday;
I walked to the shop
The bus fare in my purse
With little more
And I thought of dying
But the image of my passing
Did not help;

In the shop I looked
For the best of things
The price of which
I did not have
And I promised me
That I would have them all;
My bag was worn and open
To receive the things
I gave it to enfold
And another bag
From them for nothing
Helped me gain my joy;
I filled both bags,
My comforts for tomorrow,
With the victuals
For which I couldn't pay,
Bacon, sausages,
Cheese and chicken,
Tissues for crying
For what I was doing,
Bread and soft buns
Brown and white,
With every kind of sauce
And relish for my feasts
But I worried about
How I'd get them home;

The man came as I waddled past the door
A badge in hand he held me with my bags,
I was caught with no escape, my birthday-plan was over,
I was seventy yesterday, a different story now.

I watched the old lady taken
And I followed her and him,
That catching-man for them,
To an office of control
Where she, a simple elder,
Seventy yesterday, was detained
And I wondered
If there wasn't a better way.

ABOUT A MAN ON THE STREET

My Friend, Paul....01

Is he forty, fifty,
I don't know;
His wispy hair
hangs
beyond his shoulders
framing
a drawn-red face
and a pallid
welcome-smile;
Paul is on the street
in his best and shaking
not from drink, he says,
but from the stroke
that took his right side
leaving that side warm,
he has no feeling there
and cold looks only
at his left
surviving side;
"I'm Paul" he said,
"They call me Michael
sometimes,
they've a lot of names
for me".

My Friend, Paul....02

Adrift
In a money-swollen City,
Paul embraced his chance
To be the best he could;
The City-Rich
Engaged in shopping,
High-end shit,
To boost
A swollen ego
And Paul was left behind;
The pavement was his home
By day and mostly nights
And a 'shilling'
Sometimes bought
His nightly bed
For a few hours
Of nightmare sleep;
Paul was a good
Compliant tenant
And he made his bed
When leaving
But Paul
Was on the street.

My Friend, Paul.....03

His wave to me
was hesitant
But familiar
and it meant
a lot to me
sometimes;
Paul had become a friend
from time to time,
someone I visited
when I thought of it
at his place
on Merchants Quay;
That day,
when he waved
and I continued smoking,
he looked away
and shuffled
to his humble space;
My space was humble too
as I stood away from him,
puffing the best I could
on a chain of cigarettes,
and the best of his humility
could produce no more for him
right then of me for now;

Later, I cringed
with guilt at my rejection
of my friend;
I strolled for a while,
his obvious hurt
was gnawing at my soul.
Go back to him,
I told myself,
have you any decency left
But I could'nt go back for now.....
.....maybe another time!

MY FRIEND, PAUL....04

"How are you" I asked
and he replied
"I'm doing the best I can"
and when I asked him
"Are you taking care
of yourself", he said
"I'm doing the best I can",
his words were sparse;
Christmas
was approaching
And its spirit
was embracing me
so I said,
as I gave him
a few coins,
"I'll see you soon"
and he replied
"That will be nice"
as I walked away
with hands in warm pockets.

My Friend, Paul....05

As cold and damp
Seeped in his shoes
And misting rain
Wet his lank hair,
Paul's head sank
To his shoulders;
He shook,
Was it with cold
Or wet
Or was it drink;
"I take a drink" he said,
"sometimes
and the shaking stops
for a while
but always
it comes back,
could you stop the shaking
please for me?".
"Drink can give you shakes"
I said with sympathy
"but only if you take too much";
"I don't" he said
"because I cannot buy it
but if I could I would".
I left for a while
and strolled and shopped
and smoked, that was

one of my addictions;
I thought a lot
about what Paul had said
and knew that he had said
the truth to me;
I also knew
That there was little
Between him and me,
I had my own afflictions,
Fears to breast,
And I decided to go back;

"You're back" he said
with a chastise-smile,
" and you were shopping,
smoking maybe,
I don't smoke, you know"
And humbly
I said "Yes, I know".
"I was something once"
he said "and I was worth a lot
to many people
but, now, I'm out of life
For far too long,
could you help
to get me back?"

My Friend, Paul….06

"I had a friend
we were close
he was on the street
He had a life
Like yours once
But now he's gone".
"Yours is a gifted life,
the silver spoon,
and his was too
but only for a while;
His spoon corroded
As yours will not
And he slid
Down a helpless path
Where you will not
In your protected frame;
He had potential too
To be the best of best
But Nature's dream
Did not become for him,
Is he better, worse
than you or me
or equal,
I don't know".

My Friend Paul.....07

Summer came and went
With little rain to dampen him
The streets were a comfort-base
For his shuffle 'round with ease
And drifting was a pleasure
With the sunshine on his craw;
Always with his long coat on
Paul, one side adrift,
Redeemed the shopping trollies
For the hackneying matrons
Whose one euro meant so little
But to him a certain win;
He took his stand
From morning through to night
With a pee-break from time to time
To weather pain
And sometimes didn't make it
With no clothes to change,.....
.....that day was never easy
But he wouldn't missed his gig,
My friend was conscientious
To a driven fault.

The City's shopping throngs
In an ever-prancing drive
Saw Paul sometimes,
Sometimes not;
When they did
He met them eye-to-eye
With a weathered smile;
When they didn't
He wondered why
But manners were his strength,.....
.....A few times, though,
He muttered an unkind word.

He had some friends, a few
Who never slipped by him
Without acknowledging
His ever-presence
And he always shook them up
For his investments;
Paul had a dream
That , maybe once by fluke,
His dream, a coin of fortune,
Would be palmed to him;

He collected coins
In a tin box held by string,
His life's endeavour,
But so far the coins were dross,
A motley ragged rattle
Of his empty-reaching dreams;

Hour upon hour, day upon day,
In elements harsh and not
He plies his pan-handle craft,
An inoffensive plea for bounty
From all-comers, friend or not,
Regardless of the time and tide
And with unrelenting shuffle-zeal
He presses on undaunted for his coin.

In Memoriam

For 'Joe Kay', RIP,
(d. December, 1994)

Face the music…
I cannot find the strength
To face the day;
The music haunts me
And the tune belies my need
And anyway
I cannot see beyond tonight;
The songs become
A blind line of despair
And words have
No more meaning….
….Goodnight, Goodbye;

He drifted into sleep
And will not wake,
He lost the tune
But had the last dance.

('Joe Kay' was the temporary name given to a Dublin postman who took his own life in December, 1994 and who was not actually identified until some six months after his death)

For Ray, RIP, (D.1995)

When all the girls were gone
He left
And went his own way
Quietly,
It was his way to say goodbye;
In early days
He took a slow path
In a shy way
Seeking dream of dreams
And timelessly kept up
His trail
Through fashion-places
In search of love;
He found it many times,
A few times maybe,
Each time
A trip in ecstacy
The last as magic
As the first and more;

Estranged, he dreamed
After the ball was over
So to speak
But none were there or real,
The last and first
And all between were gone
And now he waited
Searched and died
Locked in his own embrace.

In Memoriam Pat Tierney, RIP; (d.04.01.1996)

Moon shadow,
Kissing the world goodbye
Was not my dream;
You, moon-load,
Saddled a boy with manhood
Helped by a cohort
Cocooned in surplice
And stole the tender years
And future of a child;
Why on my back,
You fucking coward,
Why, in the fragrant innocence
Of boy becoming man,
Of simple pubiscence,
Did you and you and you
Press on me
with your lusting drive;
Why, moon,
When your beams could shield,
Did you with beam on beam
Upon the back of helplessness
Take what was mine, not yours,
NOT YOURS!

I cannot find the words to say,
How could I say
That you or you or you are forgiven;
I can't forgive for if I did
I'd die before I'll die
And I will not give you
Or you or you that satisfaction;
I'll know when it's the time
And I'll decide,
Not you or you or you,
Because this life is mine!

Where is the end
Of this demeaning nightmare,
What does it mean or is there anything,
Where does it begin or is there a beginning,
The turmoil of debate on life is death,
I cannot face that death;
I can, I must,
Its mine
And anyway
What's HIV?
I wish I knew
Or do I know
That life was doomed

From its beginning;
Where is my childhood
And my dreams of youth,
Are they all gone
Or were they ever there;

I'll know
When it's the time
For my life
And I'll decide
When its to end;
I'm Pat,
I love you, Pat,
Why did it take
So long to say;
I'm Pat,
I'm dead,
What's life,…..
…..I'm fine now.

(Pat Tierney died by his own hand in a Dublin churchyard on the 4th January, 1996, his thirty-ninth birthday. He had been forced to spend his early life in an 'Industrial School' run by Catholic clergy and sanctioned and supported by the Irish State; He told his tragic story in a book entitled 'The Moon on my Back'.)

In Memoriam Thom McGinty, RIP, (D.1995)

On Grafton Street
Afterwards
The Sun shone
And the beauty people
Were as only
They can be
And the stream of life
Continued;
I knew you
Only barely
But I knew
Your time and space
And presence
And I saw you cry;
Now I walk
The street
And the Diceman's
Gone.....
.....Goodbye, Thom.

In Memoriam Jack, RIP, 18.04.2005

A moment split-time
Made him in a love-embrace,
A tiny thing,
A start of Jack to grow,
A mini-version
Of a human beauty-form;
He grew awhile inside
And kicked for life
From day to day
To being with us;
He sucked and rolled,
An embryo-form,
To face the tunnel
Of a World embrace;

A gasping pain
Warned of sadness
And a flow-fear
took control;
The safe-womb space
Was flawed for once,
Protection failed
And Jack was gone;
The womb-sack
Brought him home,
Needed here
But wanted in another place
To Heaven;
Jack, an angel-child,
Became an angel forever.

In Memoriam John McGahern, RIP, (1934-2006).

Hello, John,
Born to poor and Mammy's pain,
To be reared to Daddy's fist
And dire nothing;
Gone to school, John,
For the way to educate
To a teacher, in ideals,
To be sent away....You were!
Earlier, you were the pup
Of your beginning
Walking wooded lanes
Of the country of your baby-days;
Later, cringing at the brink
Where you cut your writing teeth,
You strolled through
The Nature-Lanes of home;
A Teacher, Educator,
embraced the frame
Of that back-time
But the Moral of
The Maidens Dancing
Shook the heavens
and readied flames of hell
For you, they said,.....
.....You paid the price!

The Scholar paid the price
When the church's Hammer
Fell on his 'sad' life
And, naturally,
As in the place you walked and wrote,
You took the crown of Joyce and others
And the quiff of Beckett and the rest;

Naturally,
You shook the mantle
of those erstwhile heroes
into the memory
of an empty chasm
where excitement,
driven by a Gaelic
Scholar-Dream,
Took awards from the far winds
To an immortal frame
With words and without dreams,
With DREAMS;

Now gone, your voice
Acclaimed in my place
And in yours,
The message of your life,
Was published to applause
In your sojourn here and after;
Your lisp-voice, a chronicle
Of a life well known,
Spoke of prison
And of freedom
Born, and brave alive,
Now dead but lives.....
......Good Night, John
And God Bless!

For John McGahern, RIP; (1934-2006).

Early
In the country
You saw
a job for life
And fought
for that;

Later
in your words
You looked
for future,
And sculpted
A new place;
In the end,
In the world of you,
A place in words
was built
And a woman-world
Was born.

FOR FRANK NASH, RIP.

Sadness awaited
Those around him, kin and not,
The many who were reached
By his entrancing soft embrace;
The boy came of a soft beginning,
The warmth of simple love
And grew from that to search horizons
For the wonder of all life;
That boy sucked
Of the wonder-breast
Of local nurture
And swelled to be what he became;
The man, again, again,
Grew more not for himself
But for the people of his place
And reached the summit of that dedication;
That human-effort man
Reached the fence, his end of being,
And in its face he was not daunted
By the prospect of his journey,…..
……He was ready to go home;

Now, the sadness has evaporated
Into the soft-mist
Of the best of memory
And the man is celebrated
For the life of him, Frank Nash,
Safe Home, Frank.

In Memoriam Emer, RIP, d. 2007

Sad thoughts abounded
When the end of beauty came;

The news was bad,
her young last breath
was taken
by her wish and hand;
She planned each step,
her trip to friends,
embrace of family,
and her leaving
and she left,
champagne-borne,
tablet-laden,
in a quiet sleep;

Her friend,
my child,
heard the news
with shock
and tears flowed loose;
The memories
of a living life,
together and apart,
swept through her heart;

Crying,
with her children close,
she sought an answer
for the end of Emer;
Sobbing,
she took her child
in a hug to her
and the boy asked
"Was she broken, Mam?'
"She was" my girl replied......

In Memoriam
Anna Maria Pattwell, RIP.

I tipped the candle over
It wasn't my fault
It was the badger in my head;
A badness took my brain
And I am lost
In a mindless maze;
I saw the badger
And a freeway
In my mind took over;
Not thinking, not being clear
Of the world or where I was,
I looked and saw a haze;
I saw that badger
And I tried my best
To think
But nothing came;

I am lost and trying to think
But my mind is gone;
I am alone fenced off
Not here at all
For me or you,….
…..I'm sorry Son.

In Memoriam Mick Lally, RIP.

Life left a Legend yesterday
And the people,
Public, private, everyone,
Lamented his too early passing,
Felt a loss in their bones,
The last trip of a journeyman;

"You took us by surprise, Mick,
You had much done, more to do";
"I was finished, well and truly finished",
He answered with a cheesy grin;
"The rest will do me good
Like many actors for a while
But I'll look out for chances
On the new-life stage that waits,
I'll surely see ye all again
At my first performance there".

His last breath spent,
Mick travelled
In his unique style
To the place set out for him
On a heavenly stage
Where waiting, "Holy God"
Was the Director
For his best endeavours yet;

"The World will miss you, Mick,"
The stages where he stepped
Are echoing and his Gaelic voice
Whispers back "Well, Holy God,
I'm not really gone at all,
Just visiting Home".

In Memoriam Jim O'Driscoll, RIP.

Blossoms
Upturned faces
Climbed to the sky
As the Sun lifted
From its bed;
The gold-orb
Spanned its light
To the world below
And dark was gone
To let him grow
And hear the flowers sing
In their angel-voice
All the colours blooming
In his wonder mind;
But a darkness
Fell too soon
On his blossom-life,
The light went out
And he went home,....
....Good Night, Jim.

Painting the Wind.....
(In Memoriam Denis Raphael Greene, RIP.)

The wind blew in
A shaggy yellow-red embrace
Of the Spring Sun
Glowing through the day
To bear the soul
Of an Island-Man away;
He had passed with the stars,
With the early Sun,
And his leaving breath
Took his life-vapour
To a non-earth place
Where he could rest in laughter;

The world, his past, is gone
To his new beginning,
A soft-sun warming the path
Of his last journey
While chilly winds
Forced collars to turn up;
Off-white clouds
Sparse in the sky
Gave way to new-lines
Of departing planes
Searching their path
On a westward journey

Past the home of his beginning
Past Valentia and beyond;

The world witnessed
The final journey
Of an Island Man
And saw him safely home.

In Loving Memory.....

Bent and shagged to death
She worked her way
Through feelings cold
And sucked inside
The frame-creation
Of an angry man;
Fucked and empty
She walked her path
Unsafe but holding
An empty dream of love
In the dead vessel
Of his non-embrace;
But she cracked
Beneath his rampant ire
And took the cash to leave
But before she left
She fucked him back
With a long blade
To send him home
In return-pain,.....
.....Then she walked
    behind his coffin
    to his grave
    in loving memory!

A Dark Place

TALKING TO MYSELF

Mumbling
Muttering
Madness
On a trip
With me
In talk
Alone,
the world around
alive with action
circles my space
and intrudes
at the fence
of my conversation
me with me
alone;

But space
engorged
abusing space
with noise,
a harshness-crowding,
must not breach
that tender fence
that holds
the safety
of my private
word with me,
my talk
with me
alone.......
.......more space is needed!

Lost in the Sadness

An urge of instinct
Swelled through the dark
As heart and soul begged
For a soft response
To an earnest cry
not seen or heard
but long foretold
in a home embrace;
Bright and airy
With the positives
Of every choice,
No real signal shone
To warn of gloom
But doom and death,
Begged as relief,
Were on the way;

How are you, friend,
Was, or so it seemed,
A perfect question
And the answer always,
The same and satisfying,
Was good enough,
That is until
The bad news came
and my friend was no more;

Could I do more
You ask in disbelief
And was I listening
Or was he hiding something,
Was it him
Or was it me?
The answer never comes
Because he's gone
And more will go that way
But me, I will remember.

TANGLE

A tangled mind-trip
In a savage-jungled mood
Spent the aged energy
Of a fast-evaporation,
Of an expiry-promise
Engraved from the birthing place,...
.....Inevitably,
The end must come!
And come it will
Despite the fight,
The stricken-powered
Angst for more,
And it will win
To take the fighter home
But where is home
Or where will he move to
When he goes over,
Will he live again?

Never fearing,
He spent his early days
In a will-borne drive
For earthly joy,
For pleasure
Beyond bounds,
But, later in decline,
He looked with conscience
To the skies
For hope of saving,.....
.....Is that the way
That it must be
Or is there, somewhere,
Another place to be?

The question remains
A dillema
For every human being
Where ever he comes from!

The End is Me

In the mind of it,
That wet dank place of it,
The desolation seeps
Like a bog-borne sump;

Sun may shine,
The fresh wind
Might lighten fog
But a dark embrace
Of a now desire
Will not let go,
the mind is bent
on its escape;

Shadows look
for a level crossing,
a way to leave in peace
or find the peace of leaving
but a sprinkle-shower comes
in time for further thought;

Why now
And why not later if at all;
A world still waits
To find a way to go,
Or not to go if going
Will let a mind remain
In place with peace,
And the shower,
A sympathy intrusion,
Saves, for now or maybe
For at least another day,
A life or two because
that's all there is to be;
Life was there before
But life is there no more
my friends;
The world is over now
For now at least.

Tipping Along

Morning breaks
But days get dark,
Despite the Sun's
Endeavours;
Empty reaches
of the mind
Yield uninvited
demon-thoughts;
Sure as hell
A lassitude,
Wished for
Or not,
Claws through
From toe to head;
Effort is needed,
Not inclined,
To fan some spark,
At least an ember
But none will show
In the current
Shadow-world,
The now-today
Is not the place to be
So where to Now?

TABLET EXPRESS

Coyote-tablets ambushed
A softened brain
Embedded in the bogland
Of a work-engaged stress,
The well-worn path
From day to day,
A cess-pool of endeavour
In a thankless world,
And the pressure took it's toll,
Not once but twice
In a medicated 'dream',
The world ended and began again
That second 'fatal' try for peace.

GUARDIAN ANGEL

A cold gloom hovered over me,
Shadowing everyone, the world;
It penetrated my soul
And I couldn't find a way
Through the haze
Of lonely-reaching;
Each cry, a siren-sound from hell,
Pressed me to the brink
And I resisted
But with weakening resolve
Looked over the edge
To a comfort-cushion in the flow
And I wanted freedom then;

Despite the conflict in my mind
A magnet-mood
Was drawing me enchanted
To a womb-like stream;
Clutching the rail and climbing
I felt the ecstacy envelop me
And I was well and feeling better
And no tomorrow could be today,
This moment, or this sense of peace
And the river-bed was swathed
In a spreadlike sheen
Held out, it seemed, for me;

Why wait,
That thought was pressing
Compelling my mind
To a final trip,
The end of misery,
Of everything,

The end of songs and silence,
Yet I waited,
Something drawing me back;
But no one's there
Or so it seems
And, yet, I feel an energy
Holding me, taking me
Back to before now
Before the pain
To the beginning;
Then I know
That now, for now,
Is better
So I will wait
And will not try again
Tonight.

To Sleep and Back

Nice to see you
Again in waking
Coming back
To the world
A misery
You tried
To leave behind
Welcome back
To the emptiness
You sought to leave;
Night provided cover
For your trip-attempt,
The dose-embracing
Batch of packet-pills,
Your clawing need
To be asleep
Away to an oblivion
Where you could not see
Or hear and where
If all had done the job
The world would let you free;

Welcome back
To see and hear
A news of life,
Not one of being
Gone for good
But being, doing
For the person that is you
And not for them;
Welcome with good luck
To a new world,
The first day's life of you
And hearty greetings,
Well-wished thoughts,
On your continuing
Return home.